100
PROMISES
and
Prayers
For
Kids

100
PROMISES
and
Prayers
For
Kids

*FS
FREEMAN-SMITH

INTRODUCTION

A Message for Parents

If your child's bookshelf is already spilling over with a happy assortment of good books for kids, congratulations—that means you're a thoughtful parent who understands the importance of reading to your child.

This little book is an important addition to your child's library. It is intended to be read by Christian parents to their young children. The text contains 100 brief chapters. Each chapter consists of a Bible promise, a brief story or lesson, kid-friendly quotations from notable Christian thinkers, a tip for kids, and a prayer.

For the next 100 days, take the time to read one chapter each night to your child, and then spend a few moments talking about the chapter's meaning. By the time you finish the book, you will have had 100 different opportunities to share God's wisdom with your son or daughter, and that's good . . . very good.

If you have been touched by God's love and His grace, then you know the joy that He has brought into your own life. Now it's your turn to share His promises with the boy or girl whom He has entrusted to your care. Happy reading! And may God richly bless you and your family now and forever.

WITH LOVE IN YOUR HEART

So these three things continue forever:
faith, hope, and love.
And the greatest of these is love.
1 Corinthians 13:13 ICB

The words of 1 Corinthians 13:13 remind us that love is God's commandment: "But now abide faith, hope, love, these three; but the greatest of these is love" (v. 13 NASB). Faith is important, of course. So is hope. But, love is more important still.

Christ loved us first, and, as Christians, we are called upon to return His love by sharing it. Today, let's share Christ's love with our families and friends. When we do, we'll discover that a loving heart is also a patient heart. And, we'll discover that the more we love, the more patient we become.

In the presence of love, miracles happen.

Robert Schuller

A little rain can strengthen a flower stem. A little love can change a life.

Max Lucado

Kid-Tip

Pray for a heart that is loving and patient, and remember that God answers prayer!

A Prayer for Today

Dear Lord, give me a heart that is filled with love, patience, and concern for others. Slow me down and calm me down so that I can see the needs of other people. And then, give me a loving heart so that I will do something about the needs that I see. Amen

THE RULE THAT'S GOLDEN

*Do for other people the same things
you want them to do for you.*
Matthew 7:12 ICB

Do you want other people to be honest with you? Of course you do. And that's why you should be honest with them. The words of Matthew 7:12 remind us that, as believers in Christ, we should treat others as we wish to be treated. And that means telling them the truth!

The Golden Rule is your tool for deciding how you will treat other people. When you use the Golden Rule as your guide for living, your words and your actions will be pleasing to other people and to God.

The Golden Rule starts at home, but it should never stop there.

Marie T. Freeman

It is one of the most beautiful compensations of life that no one can sincerely try to help another without helping herself.

Barbara Johnson

Kid-Tip

Use the Golden Rule to help you decide what to say: If you wouldn't like something said about you, then you probably shouldn't say it about somebody else!

A Prayer for Today

Dear Lord, help me remember to treat other people in the same way that I would want to be treated if I were in their shoes. The Golden Rule is Your rule, Father; I'll make it my rule, too. Amen

GOOD THINKING

Those who are pure in their thinking are happy, because they will be with God.

Matthew 5:8 NCV

Do you try to think good thoughts about your friends, your family, and yourself? The Bible says that you should. Do you lift your hopes and your prayers to God many times each day? The Bible says that you should. Do you say "no" to people who want you to do bad things or think bad thoughts? The Bible says that you should.

The Bible teaches you to guard your thoughts against things that are hurtful or wrong. So remember this: When you turn away from bad thoughts and turn instead toward God and His Son Jesus, you will be protected . . . and you will be blessed.

It is the thoughts and intents of the heart that shape a person's life.

John Eldredge

Attitude is the mind's paintbrush; it can color any situation.

Barbara Johnson

Kid-Tip

Good thoughts can lead you to some very good places . . . and bad thoughts can lead elsewhere. So guard your thoughts accordingly.

A Prayer for Today

Dear Lord, You teach me that my thoughts are important to You. Help me to think good thoughts and to do good deeds, today and every day. Amen

GOD IS LOVE

Whoever does not love does not know God,
because God is love.

1 John 4:8 ICB

The Bible tells us that God is love and that if we wish to know Him, we must have love in our hearts. Sometimes, of course, when we're tired, frustrated, or angry, it is very hard for us to be loving. Thankfully, anger and frustration are feelings that come and go, but God's love lasts forever.

If you'd like to improve your day and your life, share God's love with your family and friends. Every time you love, every time you are kind, and every time you give, God smiles.

There's nothing you can do to get Him to love you and there's nothing you can do to make Him stop.

Charles Stanley

Grin! God loves you! The rest of us will wonder what you've been up to.

Anonymous

Kid-Tip

It's good to tell your loved ones how you feel about them, but that's not enough. You should also show them how you feel with your good deeds and your kind words.

A Prayer for Today

Dear Lord, make me a person who is loving and giving. You first loved me, Father. Let me, in turn, love others, and let my behavior show them that I love them, today and forever. Amen

DAY 5

GROWING UP DAY BY DAY

*When I was a child, I spoke and thought and
reasoned as a child does.
But when I grew up, I put away childish things.*

1 Corinthians 13:11 NLT

You're growing up day by day, and it's a wonderful thing to watch. Every day, you're learning new things and doing new things. Good for you!

And when should you stop growing up? Hopefully never! That way, you'll always be learning more and doing more.

Do you think it's good to keep growing and growing and growing? If you said "yes," you're right. So remember: you're a very special person today . . . and you'll be just as special when you've grown a little bit more tomorrow.

16

No matter what we are going through, no matter how long the waiting for answers, of one thing we may be sure. God is faithful. He keeps His promises. What He starts, He finishes . . . including His perfect work in us.

Gloria Gaither

With God, it isn't who you were that matters; it's who you are becoming.

Liz Curtis Higgs

Kid-Tip

Grown-ups still have plenty to learn . . . and so do you!

A Prayer for Today

Dear Lord, thank You for letting me grow a little bit more every day. I thank You for the person I am . . . and for the person I can become. Amen

DAY 6

SHARING YOUR STUFF

God loves the person who gives cheerfully.
2 Corinthians 9:7 NLT

How many times have you heard someone say, "Don't touch that; it's mine!" If you're like most of us, you've heard those words many times and you may have even said them yourself.

The Bible tells us that it's better for us to share things than it is to keep them all to ourselves. And the Bible also tells us that when we share, it's best to do so cheerfully. So today and every day, let's share. It's the best way because it's God's way.

Nothing is really ours until we share it.

C. S. Lewis

The happiest and most joyful people are those who give money and serve.

Dave Ramsey

Kid-Tip

Too many toys? Give them away! Are you one of those lucky kids who has more toys than you can play with? If so, remember that not everyone is so lucky. Ask your parents to help you give some of your toys to children who need them more than you do.

A Prayer for Today

Dear Lord, You have given me so much. Let me share my gifts with others, and let me be a joyful and generous Christian, today and every day. Amen

IF YOU NEED HELP, ASK GOD!

*We pray that the Lord will lead
your hearts into God's love
and Christ's patience.*
2 Thessalonians 3:5 ICB

Do you need help in becoming a more patient person? If so, ask God; He's always ready, willing, and able to help. In fact, the Bible promises that when we sincerely seek God's help, He will give us the things we need.

So, if you want to become a better person, bow your head and start praying about it. And then rest assured that with God's help, you can change for the better . . . and you will!

God makes prayer as easy as possible for us. He's completely approachable and available, and He'll never mock or upbraid us for bringing our needs before Him.

Shirley Dobson

Some people think God does not like to be troubled with our constant asking. But, the way to trouble God is not to come at all.

D. L. Moody

Kid-Tip

Don't be too hard on yourself: you don't have to be perfect to be wonderful. God loves you . . . and you should too.

A Prayer for Today

Dear Lord, I have so much to learn and so many ways to improve myself, but You love me just as I am. Thank You for Your love and for Your Son. And, help me to become the person that You want me to become. Amen

PATIENCE IS

Always be humble and gentle.
Be patient and accept each other with love.
Ephesians 4:2 ICB

The dictionary defines the word "patience" as "the ability to be calm, tolerant, and understanding." Here's what that means: the word "calm" means being in control of your emotions (not letting your emotions control you). The word "tolerant" means being kind and considerate to people who are different from you. And, the word "understanding" means being able to put yourself in another person's shoes.

If you can be calm, tolerant, and understanding, you will be the kind of person whose good deeds are a blessing to your family and friends. They will appreciate your good deeds, and so will God.

Two signposts of faith: "Slow Down" and "Wait Here."

Charles Stanley

Patience is a virtue that carries a lot of wait.

Anonymous

Kid-Tip

Since you want other people to be patient with you, you should be patient with them, too.

A Prayer for Today

Dear Lord, sometimes it's hard to be a patient person, and that's exactly when I should try my hardest to be patient. Help me to follow Your commandments by being a patient, loving Christian, even when it's hard. Amen

HOW WOULD JESUS BEHAVE?

Love other people just as Christ loved us.
Ephesians 5:2 ICB

If you're not sure whether something is right or wrong—kind or unkind—ask yourself a simple question: "How would Jesus behave if He were here?" The answer to that question will tell you what to do.

Jesus was perfect, but we are not. Still, we must try as hard as we can to do the best that we can. When we do, we will love others, just as Christ loves us.

There is not a single thing that Jesus cannot change, control, and conquer because He is the living Lord.

Franklin Graham

The only source of Life is the Lord Jesus Christ.

Oswald Chambers

Kid-Tip

Learning about Jesus: Start learning about Jesus, and keep learning about Him as long as you live. His story never grows old, and His teachings never fail.

A Prayer for Today

Dear Lord, let me use Jesus as my guide for living. When I have questions about what to do or how to act, let me behave as He behaved. When I do, I will share His love with my family, with my friends, and with the world. Amen

OBEY THE RULES

Here is my final advice:
Honor God and obey his commands.
Ecclesiastes 12:13 ICB

If you're old enough to know right from wrong, then you're old enough to do something about it. In other words, you should always try to obey your family's rules.

How can you tell "the right thing" from "the wrong thing"? By listening carefully to your parents, that's how.

The more self-control you have, the easier it is to obey your parents. Why? Because, when you learn to think first and do things next, you avoid making silly mistakes. So here's what you should do: First, slow down long enough to listen to your parents. Then, do the things that you know your parents want you to do.

Face facts: your family has rules . . . and it's better for everybody when you obey them.

God uses ordinary people who are obedient to Him to do extraordinary things.

John Maxwell

Obedience is the outward expression of your love of God.

Henry Blackaby

Kid-Tip

Be patient, and follow the rules . . . even if you don't like some of the rules that you're supposed to follow, follow them anyway.

A Prayer for Today

Dear Lord, when I play by Your rules, You bless my life. But, when I disobey Your rules, I suffer the consequences. Help me obey You and my parents . . . starting right now! Amen

DAY 11

BE KIND TO EVERYONE

Show respect for all people.
Love the brothers and sisters of God's family.
1 Peter 2:17 ICB

Who deserves our respect? Grown-ups? Of course. Teachers? Certainly. Family members? Yes. Friends? That's right, but it doesn't stop there. The Bible teaches us to treat all people with respect.

Respect for others is habit-forming: the more we do it, the easier it becomes. So start practicing right now. Say lots of kind words and do lots of kind things, because when it comes to kindness and respect, practice makes perfect.

When you launch an act of kindness out into the crosswinds of life, it will blow kindness back to you.

Dennis Swanberg

When we do little acts of kindness that make life more bearable for someone else, we are walking in love as the Bible commands us.

Barbara Johnson

Kid-Tip

Make sure that you show proper respect for everyone, even if that person happens to be different from you. It's easy to make fun of people who seem different . . . but it's wrong.

A Prayer for Today

Dear Lord, help me to be kind to everyone I meet. Help me to be respectful to all people, not just teachers and parents. Help me to say kind words and do good deeds, today and every day. Amen

DAY 12

CHURCH IS A WONDERFUL PLACE

*Don't you realize that all of you together
are the temple of God and that
the Spirit of God lives in you?*

1 Corinthians 3:16 NLT

When your parents take you to church, are you pleased to go? Hopefully so. After all, church is a wonderful place to learn about God's rules.

The church belongs to God just as surely as you belong to God. That's why the church is a good place to learn about God and about His Son Jesus.

So when your mom and dad take you to church, remember this: church is a fine place to be . . . and you're lucky to be there.

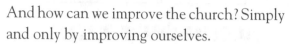

And how can we improve the church? Simply and only by improving ourselves.

A. W. Tozer

Only participation in the full life of a local church builds spiritual muscle.

Rick Warren

Kid-Tip

Forget the Excuses: If somebody starts making up reasons not to go to church, don't pay any attention . . . even if that person is you!

A Prayer for Today

Dear Lord, thank You for my church. When I am at church, I will be generous, kind, well-behaved, and respectful. And when I am not at church, I will act the same way. Amen

DAY 13

KEEP ON TRYING

Be on guard. Stand true to what you believe.
Be courageous. Be strong.
1 Corinthians 16:13 NLT

When things don't turn out right, it's easy for most of us to give up. But usually, it's wrong. Why are we tempted to give up so quickly? Perhaps we're afraid that we might embarrass ourselves if we tried hard but didn't succeed.

Here's something to remember: if you're having a little trouble getting something done, don't get mad, don't get frustrated, don't get discouraged, and don't give up. Just keep trying and keep believing in yourself.

When you try hard you can do amazing things . . . but if you quit at the first sign of trouble, you'll miss out. So here's a good rule to follow: when you have something that you want to finish, be brave enough (and wise enough) to finish it.

God never gives up on you, so don't you ever give up on Him.

Marie T. Freeman

Perseverance is more than endurance. It is endurance combined with absolute assurance and certainty that what we are looking for is going to happen.

Oswald Chambers

Kid-Tip

If things don't work out at first, don't quit. If you never try, you'll never know how good you can be.

A Prayer for Today

Dear Lord, sometimes I feel like giving up. When I feel that way, help me do the right thing . . . and help me finish the work You want me to do. Amen

DAY 14

DON'T WORRY

Give all your worries and cares to God,
for he cares about what happens to you.

1 Peter 5:6 NLT

If you're feeling upset, what should you do? Well, you should talk to your parents and there's something else you can do: you can pray about it.

If there is a person you don't like, you should pray for a forgiving heart. If there is something you're worried about, you should ask God to give you comfort. And as you pray more, you'll discover that God is always near and that He's always ready to hear from you. So don't worry about things; pray about them. God is waiting patiently to hear from you . . . and He's ready to listen NOW!

Worry does not empty tomorrow of its sorrow; it empties today of its strength.

Corrie ten Boom

Worry is the senseless process of cluttering up tomorrow's opportunities with leftover problems from today.

Barbara Johnson

Kid-Tip

If you're worried about something, talk to your parents and pray to God. When you do these things, you'll feel better in a hurry.

A Prayer for Today

Dear Lord, when I am worried, I know where to turn for help: to those who love me, and to You. Thank You, for the people who love and care for me, and thank You, Lord, for Your love. Because of that love, I have hope and assurance for this day and every day. Amen

DAY 15

SET THE EXAMPLE

*You are young, but do not let anyone treat you
as if you were not important. Be an example to
show the believers how they should live.
Show them with your words,
with the way you live, with your love,
with your faith, and with your pure life.*
1 Timothy 4:12 ICB

What kind of example are you? Are you the
kind of person who shows other people what
it means to be kind and forgiving? Hopefully
so!!!

How hard is it to say a kind word? Not
very! How hard is it to accept someone's
apology? Usually not too hard. So today, be
a good example for others to follow. Because
God needs people like you who are willing
to stand up and be counted for Him. That's
exactly the kind of example you should try
to be.

In our faith we follow in someone's steps. In our faith we leave footprints to guide others. It's the principle of discipleship.

Max Lucado

We urgently need people who encourage and inspire us to move toward God and away from the world's enticing pleasures.

Jim Cymbala

Kid-Tip

Your friends are watching: so be the kind of example that God wants you to be—be a good example.

A Prayer for Today

Lord, make me a good example to my family and friends. Let the things that I say and do show everybody what it means to be a good person and a good Christian. Amen

IT'S BETTER TO BE PATIENT

Patience is better than strength.
Proverbs 16:32 ICB

In the Book of Proverbs, we are told that patience is a very good thing. But for most of us, patience can also be a very hard thing. After all, we have many things that we want, and we want them NOW! But the Bible tells us that we must learn to wait patiently for the things that God has in store for us.

Are you having trouble being patient? If so, remember that patience takes practice, and lots of it, so keep trying. And if you make a mistake, don't be too upset. After all, if you're going to be a really patient person, you shouldn't just be patient with others; you should also be patient with yourself.

The challenge before us is to have faith in God, and the hardest part of faith is waiting.

Jim Cymbala

If only we could be as patient with other people as God is with us!

Jim Gallery

Kid-Tip

Take a deep breath, a very deep breath: if you think you're about to say or do something you'll regret later, slow down and take a deep breath, or two deep breaths, or ten, or . . . well, you get the point.

A Prayer for Today

Dear Lord, the Bible tells me that it's better to be patient than impulsive. Help me to slow myself down so I can make better decisions today and every day. Amen

DAY 17

BEING A TRUSTWORTHY FRIEND

*Tell each other the truth because
we all belong to each other . . .*
Ephesians 4:25 ICB

All genuine friendships are built upon both honesty and trust. Without trust, friends soon drift apart. But with trust, friends can stay friends for a lifetime.

As Christians, we should always try to be trustworthy, encouraging, loyal friends. And, we should be thankful for the people who are loyal friends to us. When we treat other people with honesty and respect, we not only make more friends, but we also keep the friendships we've already made.

Do you want friends you can trust? Then start by being a friend they can trust. That's the way to make your friendships strong, stronger, and strongest!

The best times in life are made a thousand times better when shared with a dear friend.

Luci Swindoll

Inasmuch as anyone pushes you nearer to God, he or she is your friend.

Barbara Johnson

Kid-Tip

Lies tear down trust: one of the best ways to destroy even a friendship is to lie to your friend . . . so don't do it!

A Prayer for Today

Dear Lord, help me to be an honest friend. Since I want other people to be truthful with me, let me be truthful with them, today and every day. Amen

KINDNESS STARTS WITH YOU!

We must not become tired of doing good.
We will receive our harvest of eternal life
at the right time. We must not give up!

Galatians 6:9 ICB

If you're waiting for other people to be nice to you before you're nice to them, you've got it backwards. Kindness starts with you! You see, you can never control what other people will say or do, but you can control your own behavior.

The Bible tells us that we should never stop doing good deeds as long as we live. Kindness is God's way, and it should be our way, too. Starting now!

As you're rushing through life, take time to stop a moment, look into people's eyes, say something kind, and try to make them laugh!

Barbara Johnson

Be so preoccupied with good deeds that you haven't room in your heart for bad deeds.

E. Stanley Jones

Kid-Tip

Kindness should be part of our lives every day, not just on the days when we feel good. Don't try to be kind some of the time, and don't try to be kind to some of the people you know . . . be kind to ALL of the people you know.

A Prayer for Today

Dear Lord, help me to remember that it is always my job to treat others with kindness and respect. Make the Golden Rule my rule and make Your Word my guidebook for the way I treat other people. Amen

DAY 19

MAKING OTHER PEOPLE FEEL BETTER!

Let us think about each other and help each other to show love and do good deeds.
Hebrews 10:24 ICB

When other people are sad, what can we do? We can do our best to cheer them up by showing kindness and love.

The Bible tells us that we must care for each other, and when everybody is happy, that's an easy thing to do. But, when people are sad, for whatever reason, it's up to us to speak a kind word or to offer a helping hand.

Do you know someone who is discouraged or sad? If so, perhaps it's time to take matters into your own hands. Think of something you can do to cheer that person up . . . and then do it! You'll make two people happy.

No matter how crazy or nutty your life has seemed, God can make something strong and good out of it. He can help you grow wide branches for others to use as shelter.

Barbara Johnson

Encouraging others means helping people, looking for the best in them, and trying to bring out their positive qualities.

John Maxwell

Kid-Tip

If you want to cheer someone up but can't think of something to say or do, try drawing a picture or writing a note.

A Prayer for Today

Dear Lord, make me a loving, encouraging Christian. And let my love for Jesus be reflected through the kindness that I show to those who need the healing touch of the Master's hand. Amen

YOU CAN'T PLEASE EVERYBODY

Do you think I am trying to make people
accept me? No, God is the One I am trying to
please. Am I trying to please people?
If I still wanted to please people,
I would not be a servant of Christ.

Galatians 1:10 NCV

Are you one of those people who tries to please everybody in sight? If so, you'd better watch out! After all, if you worry too much about pleasing your friends, you may not worry enough about pleasing God.

Whom will you try to please today: your God or your pals? The answer to that question should be simple. Your first job is to obey God's rules . . . and that means obeying your parents, too!

You should forget about trying to be popular with everybody and start trying to be popular with God Almighty.

Sam Jones

If you try to be everything to everybody, you will end up being nothing to anybody.

Vance Havner

Kid-Tip

Please God first. Then, work very hard to please your parents.

A Prayer for Today

Dear Lord, help me remember that I don't have to please everybody . . . but that I should always try to please You! Amen

GOD HAS RULES

*We can be sure that we know God
if we obey his commands.*

1 John 2:3 NCV

God has rules, and He wants you to obey them. He wants you to be fair, honest, and kind. He wants you to behave yourself, and He wants you to respect your parents. God has other rules, too, and you'll find them in a very special book: the Bible.

With a little help from your parents, you can figure out God's rules. And then, it's up to you to live by them. When you do, everybody will be pleased—you'll be pleased, your parents will be pleased . . . and God will be pleased, too.

The golden rule to follow to obtain spiritual understanding is not one of intellectual pursuit, but one of obedience.

Oswald Chambers

The surest evidence of our love to Christ is obedience to the laws of Christ. Love is the root, obedience is the fruit.

Matthew Henry

Kid-Tip

Obeying God? Yes! What about all those rules you learn about in the Bible? Well, those aren't just any old rules—they're God's rules. And you should behave—and obey—accordingly.

A Prayer for Today

Dear Lord, I trust You, and I know that Your rules are good for me. I will do my best to obey You, even when it's hard. Amen

DAY 22

ANGER GETS IN THE WAY

My dear brothers, always be willing to listen and slow to speak. Do not become angry easily. Anger will not help you live a good life as God wants.

James 1:19 ICB

In the Book of James, we learn that God has a "good life" that He wants each of us to live. But if we lose patience and become angry with others, our own anger can interfere with God's plans.

Do you want the good life that God has planned for you? If so, don't let your own anger get in the way. In other words, don't interfere with your own happiness. Instead, calm down and get ready for the wonderful life that God has promised to those whose hearts are filled with patience and with love.

When you lose your temper . . . you lose.

Marie T. Freeman

Get rid of the poison of built-up anger and the acid of long-term resentment.

Charles Swindoll

Kid-Tip

Think carefully . . . make that very carefully! If you're a little angry, think carefully before you speak. If you're very angry, think very carefully. Otherwise, you might say something in anger that you would regret later.

A Prayer for Today

Dear Lord, when I am not patient, remind me that it's better to stop and think things through than it is to rush ahead without thinking. Make me a patient person, Lord, and fill me with consideration for others and love for You. Amen

WHEN YOU MAKE MISTAKES

*Therefore, if anyone is in Christ, he is a new
creation; the old has gone, the new has come!*
2 Corinthians 5:17 NIV

Are you perfect? Certainly not! No matter
how hard you try to do the right thing, you're
bound to mistakes every once in a while . . .
everybody does.

When you make a mistake, what should
you do about it? Here are two things you
should do:

1. Try very hard to learn something from
your mistake; that way, you won't make that
same mistake again.

2. If you have hurt someone—or if you
have disobeyed God—you must ask for forgiveness. That means saying you're sorry to
the person you hurt . . . and it also means
saying you're sorry to God.

Father, take our mistakes and turn them into opportunities.

Max Lucado

God is able to take mistakes, when they are committed to Him, and make of them something for our good and for His glory.

Ruth Bell Graham

Kid-Tip

Fix it sooner rather than later: If you make a mistake, the time to make things better is now, not later! The sooner you admit your mistake, the better.

A Prayer for Today

Dear Lord, sometimes I make mistakes. When I do, forgive me, Father. And help me learn from my mistakes so that I can be a better person and a better example to my friends and family. Amen

PRAY!
GOD IS LISTENING

The earnest prayer of a righteous person has great power and wonderful results.

James 5:16 NLT

If you are upset, pray about it. If you're having trouble telling the truth, ask God to help you. If there is ever a person you don't like, pray for a forgiving heart. If there is ever something you're worried about, ask God to comfort you. As you pray more, you'll discover that God is always near and that He's always ready to hear from you. So don't worry about things; pray about them. Remember: God is waiting . . . and listening!

Prayer accomplishes more than anything else.

Bill Bright

The story of every great Christian achievement is the history of answered prayer.

E. M. Bounds

Kid-Tip

Pray early and often. One way to make sure that your heart is in tune with God is to pray often. The more you talk to God, the more He will talk to you.

A Prayer for Today

Father, help me remember the importance of prayer. You always hear my prayers, God; let me always pray them! Amen

GOD KNOWS THE HEART

*I am the Lord, and I can look into
a person's heart.*
Jeremiah 17:10 ICB

You can try to keep secrets from other people, but you can't keep secrets from God. God knows what you think and what you do. And, if you want to please God, you must start with good intentions and a kind heart.

If your heart tells you not to do something, don't do it! If your conscience tells you that something is wrong, stop! If you feel ashamed by something you've done, don't do it ever again! You can keep secrets from other people some of the time, but God is watching all of the time, and He sees everything, including your heart.

Our actions are seen by people, but our motives are monitored by God.

Franklin Graham

There's not much you can't achieve or endure if you know God is walking by your side. Just remember: Someone knows, and Someone cares.

Bill Hybels

Kid-Tip

That little voice inside your head . . . is called your conscience. Listen to it; it's usually right!

A Prayer for Today

Dear Lord, other people see me from the outside, but You know my heart. Let my heart be pure, and let me listen to the voice that You have placed there, today and always. Amen

HOW PATIENT WOULD JESUS BE?

Let me give you a new command:
Love one another. In the same way
I loved you, you love one another.
John 13:34 MSG

If you've lost patience with someone, or if you're angry, take a deep breath and then ask yourself a simple question: "How would Jesus behave if He were here?" The answer to that question will tell you what to do.

Jesus was quick to speak kind words, and He was quick to forgive others. We must do our best to be like Him. When we do, we will be patient, loving, understanding, and kind.

Jesus loves me! This I know, for the Bible tells me so. Little ones to him belong; they are weak, but he is strong. Yes, Jesus loves me! Yes, Jesus loves me! Yes, Jesus loves me! The Bible tells me so.

Anna B. Warner and Susan Warner

Jesus: the proof of God's love.

Philip Yancey

Kid-Tip

Do the thing that you think Jesus would do. And, of course, don't do something if you think that He wouldn't do it.

A Prayer for Today

Dear Lord, let me use Jesus as my example for living. When I have questions about what to do or how to act, let me behave as He behaved. When I do so, I will be patient, loving, and kind, not just today, but every day. Amen

JESUS IS YOUR FRIEND

This is my commandment,
That ye love one another, as I have loved you.
Greater love hath no man than this,
that a man lay down his life for his friends.
John 15:12-13 KJV

Whether you realize it or not, you already have a relationship with Jesus. Hopefully, it's a close relationship! Why? Because the friendship you form with Jesus will help you every day of your life . . . and beyond!

You can either choose to invite Him into your heart, or you can ignore Him altogether. Welcome Him today—and while you're at it, encourage your friends and family members to do the same.

I have a Friend in high places.

Anonymous

If you come to Christ, you will always have the option of an ever-present friend. You don't have to dial long-distance. He'll be with you every step of the way.

Bill Hybels

Kid-Tip

What a friend you have in Jesus: Jesus loves you, and He offers you eternal life with Him in heaven. Welcome Him into your heart. Now!

A Prayer for Today

Dear Lord, today I will trust Jesus. I will look to Him as my Savior, and I will follow in His footsteps. I will count Him as my dearest friend. Amen

WHAT WOULD JESUS SAY?

So Jesus said to the Jews who believed in him,
"If you continue to obey my teaching,
you are truly my followers."
John 8:31 ICB

If you are tempted to say something that isn't true, stop and ask yourself a simple question: "What would Jesus say if He were here?" The answer to that question will tell you what to say.

Jesus told His followers that the truth would make them free. As believers, we must do our best to know the truth and to tell it. When we do, we behave as our Savior behaved, and that's exactly how God wants us to behave.

A disciple is a follower of Christ. That means you take on His priorities as your own. His agenda becomes your agenda. His mission becomes your mission.

Charles Stanley

In the dark? Follow the Son.

Anonymous

Kid-Tip

Learn from your Bible: Start learning about Jesus, and keep learning about Him as long as you live. His story never grows old, and His teachings never fail.

A Prayer for Today

Dear Lord, the Bible is Your gift to me. Let me use it, let me trust it, and let me obey it, today and every day that I live. Amen

SOONER OR LATER, THE TRUTH COMES OUT!

*Everything that is hidden will be shown.
Everything that is secret will be made known.*
Luke 12:2 ICB

How often do lies stay hidden? Not very often. Usually, the truth has a way of coming out, and usually it comes out sooner rather than later. That's one of the reasons that it's so silly to tell lies: lying simply doesn't work!

Truth, on the other hand, works extremely well. When you tell the truth, you don't have to remember what you said, and there's nothing bad for other people to find out. So do yourself a favor and get into the habit of telling the truth about everything. Otherwise, you'll be letting yourself in for a whole lot of trouble, and you'll be letting yourself in for it soon!

Every decision God makes is a good and right decision, so we can be certain that every decision God makes regarding us will be a right one.

Bill Hybels

Every experience God gives us, every person he brings into our lives, is the perfect preparation for the future that only he can see.

Corrie ten Boom

Kid-Tip

Keeping lies hidden is usually impossible, so why even try?

A Prayer for Today

Dear Lord, sooner or later, the truth has a way of coming out. So give me the wisdom and the courage to tell the truth in the very beginning. The truth is Your way, Lord; let it be my way, too. Amen

TEAMWORK WORKS!

*A kingdom that is divided cannot continue,
and a family that is divided cannot continue.*

Mark 3:24-25 NCV

Helping other people can be fun! When you help others, you feel better about yourself—and you'll know that God approves of what you're doing.

A kingdom that is divided cannot continue, and a family that is divided cannot continue.

When you learn how to cooperate with your family and friends, you'll soon discover that it's more fun when everybody works together.

So do everybody a favor: learn better ways to share and better ways to cooperate. It's the right thing to do.

One person working together doesn't accomplish much. Success is the result of people pulling together to meet common goals.

John Maxwell

Cooperation is a two-way street, but for too many, it's the road less traveled.

Marie T. Freeman

Kid-Tip

Cooperation pays: When you cooperate with your friends and family, you'll feel good about yourself—and your family and friends will feel good about you, too.

A Prayer for Today

Dear Lord, help me learn to be kind, courteous, and cooperative with my family and with my friends. Amen

BE KIND TO EVERYBODY!

Let everyone see that you are gentle and kind.
The Lord is coming soon.

Philippians 4:5 NCV

An attitude of kindness starts in your heart and works its way out from there.

Do you listen to your heart when it tells you to be kind to other people? Hopefully, you do. After all, lots of people in the world aren't as fortunate as you are—and some of these folks are living very near you.

Ask your parents to help you find ways to do nice things for other people. And don't forget that everybody needs love, kindness, and respect, so you should always be ready to share those things, too.

As you're rushing through life, take time to stop a moment, look into people's eyes, say something kind, and try to make them laugh!

Barbara Johnson

When you extend hospitality to others, you're not trying to impress people, you're trying to reflect God to them.

Max Lucado

Kid-Tip

Kindness is contagious—make sure that your family and friends catch it from you!

A Prayer for Today

Lord, it's easy to be kind to some people and difficult to be kind to others. Let me be kind to all people so that I might follow in the footsteps of Your Son. Amen

CELEBRATE LIFE

Celebrate God all day, every day.
I mean, revel in him!

Philippians 4:4 MSG

Life is a gift from God. Your job is to unwrap that gift, to use it wisely, and to give thanks to the Giver.

Are you going to treat this day (and every one hereafter) as a special gift to be enjoyed and celebrated? You should—and if you really want to please God, that's exactly what you will do.

Our thoughts, not our circumstances, determine our happiness.

John Maxwell

One of the great needs in the church today is for every Christian to become enthusiastic about his faith in Jesus Christ.

Billy Graham

It is a remarkable thing that some of the most optimistic and enthusiastic people you will meet are those who have been through intense suffering.

Warren Wiersbe

Kid-Tip

If you don't feel like celebrating, start counting your blessings. Before long, you'll realize that you have plenty of reasons to celebrate.

A Prayer for Today

Lord, You have given me the gift of life. I will treasure it and celebrate it. Amen

THE GIFT OF CONTENTMENT

I've learned by now to be quite content whatever my circumstances. I'm just as happy with little as with much, with much as with little. I've found the recipe for being happy whether full or hungry, hands full or hands empty.

Philippians 4:11-12 MSG

Where can we find contentment? Is it a result of being wealthy or famous? Nope. Genuine contentment is a gift from God to those who trust Him and follow His commandments.

If we don't find contentment in God, we will never find it anywhere else. But, if we seek Him and obey Him, we will be blessed with joyful, peaceful, meaningful lives. When God dwells at the center of our lives, peace and contentment will belong to us just as surely as we belong to God.

When we do what is right, we have content-ment, peace, and happiness.

Beverly LaHaye

Make God's will the focus of your life day by day. If you seek to please Him and Him alone, you'll find yourself satisfied with life.

Kay Arthur

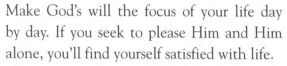

Kid-Tip

If you want to be contented . . . you should obey the rules you find in God's Word, you should obey your parents, and you should learn to trust that quiet voice that tells you right from wrong (that voice is called your conscience, and you should listen to it).

A Prayer for Today

Dear Lord, when I welcome Jesus into my heart, and when I obey Your commandments, I will be contented. Help me to trust Your Word and follow Your Son always. Amen

JUDGING OTHERS

Don't pick on people, jump on their failures,
criticize their faults—unless, of course,
you want the same treatment.
That critical spirit has a way of boomeranging.
Matthew 7:1-2 MSG

Here's something worth thinking about: If you judge other people harshly, God will judge you in the same way. But that's not all (thank goodness!). The Bible also promises that if you forgive other people, you, too, will be forgiven.

Are you tempted to blame people, criticize people, or judge people? If so, remember this: God is already judging what people do, and He doesn't need—or want—your help.

Judging draws the judgment of others.

Catherine Marshall

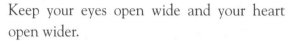

Keep your eyes open wide and your heart open wider.

Criswell Freeman

Kid-Tip

If you're setting yourself up to be the judge and jury over other people, watch out! God will judge you in the same way you judge them. So don't be too hard on other people (unless, of course, you want God to be exactly that hard on you).

A Prayer for Today

Lord, it's so easy to judge other people, but it's also easy to misjudge them. Only You can judge a human heart, Lord, so let me love my friends and neighbors, and let me help them, but never let me judge them. Amen

THINK FIRST, SPEAK LATER

The wise accumulate knowledge—
a true treasure; know-it-alls talk too much—
a sheer waste.

Proverbs 10:14 MSG

When we become frustrated or tired, it's easier to speak first and think second. But that's not the best way to talk to people. The Bible tells us that "a good person's words will help many others." But if our words are to be helpful, we must put some thought into them.

The next time you're tempted to say something unkind, remember that your words can and should be helpful to others, not hurtful. God wants to use you to make this world a better place, and He will use the things that you say to help accomplish that goal . . . if you let Him.

Giving encouragement to others is a most welcome gift, for the results of it are lifted spirits, increased self-worth, and a hopeful future.

Florence Littauer

He climbs highest who helps another up.

Zig Ziglar

Kid-Tip

When talking to other people, ask yourself this question: "How helpful can I be?"

A Prayer for Today

Dear Lord, I want my words to help other people. Let me choose my words carefully so that when I speak, the world is a better place because of the things I have said. Amen

THE BLAME GAME

*People with integrity have firm footing,
but those who follow crooked paths
will slip and fall.*

Proverbs 10:9 NLT

When something goes wrong, do you look for somebody to blame? And do you try to blame other people even if you're the one who made the mistake? Hopefully not!

It's silly to try to blame other people for your own mistakes, so don't do it.

If you've done something you're ashamed of, don't look for somebody to blame; look for a way to say, "I'm sorry, and I won't make that same mistake again."

You'll never win the blame game, so why even bother to play?

Marie T. Freeman

Instead of looking for someone to blame, look for something to fix, and then get busy fixing it.

Jim Gallery

Kid-Tip

Don't play the blame game: it's very tempting to blame others when you make mistakes or say something that isn't true. But it's more honest to look in the mirror first.

A Prayer for Today

Dear Lord, when I make a mistake, I want to admit it. Help me not blame others for the mistakes that I make. And when I make a mistake, help me to learn from it. Amen

DAY 37

CHEERFULNESS NOW

A happy heart is like a continual feast.
Proverbs 15:15 NCV

What is a continual feast? It's a little bit like a non-stop birthday party: fun, fun, and more fun! The Bible tells us that a cheerful heart can make life like a continual feast, and that's something worth working for.

Where does cheerfulness begin? It begins inside each of us; it begins in the heart. So today and every day, let's be thankful to God for His blessings, and let's show our thanks by sharing good cheer wherever we go. This old world needs all the cheering up it can get . . . and so do we!

When we bring sunshine into the lives of others, we're warmed by it ourselves. When we spill a little happiness, it splashes on us.

Barbara Johnson

God is good, and heaven is forever. And if those two facts don't cheer you up, nothing will.

Marie T. Freeman

Kid-Tip

Cheer up somebody else. Find somebody else who needs cheering up, too. Then, do your best to brighten that person's day.

A Prayer for Today

Dear Lord, make me a cheerful Christian. Today, let me celebrate my blessings and my life; let me be quick to smile and slow to become angry. And, let Your love shine in me and through me. Amen

STOP AND THINK

A wise person's mind tells him what to say.
Proverbs 16:23 ICB

When we lose control of our emotions, we do things that we shouldn't do. Sometimes, we throw tantrums. How silly! Other times we pout or whine. Too bad!

The Bible tells us that it is foolish to become angry and that it is wise to remain calm. That's why we should learn to slow down and to think about things before we do them.

Do you want to make life better for yourself and for your family? Then be patient and think things through. Stop and think before you do things, not after. It's the wise thing to do.

Waiting on God is the same as walking with God toward exciting new rooms of potential and service.

Susan Lenzkes

There is no place for faith if we expect God to fulfill immediately what he promises.

John Calvin

Kid-Tip

Tantrums? No way! If you think you might lose your temper, stop and catch your breath, and walk away if you must. It's better to walk away than it is to let your temper control you.

A Prayer for Today

Dear Lord, I can be so impatient, and I can become so angry. Calm me down, Lord, and make me a patient, forgiving Christian, today and every day of my life. Amen

WORDS ARE IMPORTANT

Pleasant words are like a honeycomb.
They make a person happy and healthy.
Proverbs 16:24 ICB

When we become angry, we may say things that are hurtful to other people. But when we strike out at others with the intention to hurt them, we are not doing God's will. God intends that His children treat others with patience, kindness, dignity, and respect. As Christians, we must do our best to obey our Creator.

Are you tempted to say an unkind word? Don't! Words are important, and once you say them, you can't call them back. But if you're wise, you won't need to!

Attitude and the spirit in which we communicate are as important as the words we say.

Charles Stanley

We do have the ability to encourage or discourage each other with the words we say. In order to maintain a positive mood, our hearts must be in good condition.

Annie Chapman

Kid-Tip

Stop, think, then speak: If you want to make your words useful instead of hurtful, don't open your mouth until you've turned on your brain and given it time to warm up.

A Prayer for Today

Dear Lord, make me a person of patience and kindness. Make the things that I say and do helpful to others, so that through me, they might see You. Amen

DAY 40

THE TROUBLE WITH GOSSIP

A person who gossips ruins friendships.
Proverbs 16:28 ICB

Do you know what gossip is? It's when we say bad things about people who are not around to hear us. When we say bad things about other people, we hurt them and we hurt ourselves. That's why the Bible tells us that gossip is wrong.

When we say things that we don't want other people to know we said, we're being somewhat dishonest, but if the things we say aren't true, we're being very dishonest. Either way, we have done something that we will regret later.

So do yourself a big favor: don't gossip. It's a waste of words, and it's the wrong thing to do. You'll feel better about yourself if you don't gossip about other people. So don't!

The cost of gossip always exceeds its worth.

Marie T. Freeman

Words. Do you fully understand their power? Can any of us really grasp the mighty force behind the things we say? Do we stop and think before we speak, considering the potency of the words we utter?

Joni Eareckson Tada

Kid-Tip

Don't say something behind someone's back that you wouldn't say to that person's face.

A Prayer for Today

Lord, make me a person who says the same things to other people that I say about them. Make my words helpful, encouraging, and true. And let the light of Christ shine in me and through me, today and forever. Amen

DAY 41

LOVING EVERYBODY (INCLUDING YOURSELF)

Above all, love each other deeply,
because love covers a multitude of sins.
1 Peter 4:8 NIV

The Bible teaches you this lesson: You should love everybody—and the word "everybody" includes yourself. Do you treat yourself with honor and respect? You should. After all, God created you in a very special way, and He loves you very much. And if God thinks you are amazing and wonderful, shouldn't you think about yourself in the same way?

So remember this: God wants you to love everybody, including the person you see when you look in the mirror. And one more thing: when you learn how to respect the person in the mirror, you'll be better at respecting other people, too.

A little rain can strengthen a flower stem. A little love can change a life.

Max Lucado

Love starts and stops with God.

Charles Stanley

The best use of life is love. The best expression of love is time. The best time to love is now.

Rick Warren

Kid-Tip

God loves you . . . and you should too.

A Prayer for Today

Dear Lord, Your love is so wonderful that I can't really imagine it, but I can share it . . . and I will . . . today and every day. Amen

DAY 42

GOD LOOKS ON THE INSIDE

God judges persons differently than humans do.
Men and women look at the face;
God looks into the heart.

1 Samuel 16:7 MSG

Other people see you from the outside, and sometimes people will judge you by the way you look. But God doesn't care how you look on the outside. Why? Because God is wiser than that; God cares about what you are on the inside—God sees your heart.

If you're like most people, you'll worry a little bit about the way you look (or maybe you'll worry a lot about it). But please don't worry too much about your appearance!

How you look on the outside isn't important . . . but how you feel on the inside is important. So don't worry about trying to impress other people.

Fashion is an enduring testimony to the fact that we live quite consciously before the eyes of others.

John Eldredge

Outside appearances, things like the clothes you wear or the car you drive, are important to other people but totally unimportant to God. Trust God.

Marie T. Freeman

Kid-Tip

Beauty on the outside isn't important . . . beauty on the inside is.

A Prayer for Today

Dear Lord, You know my heart. Help me to say things, to do things, and to think things that are pleasing to You. Amen

DON'T LOSE YOUR TEMPER

*And be careful that when you get on each
other's nerves you don't snap at each other.
Look for the best in each other,
and always do your best to bring it out.*

1 Thessalonians 5:15 MSG

Temper tantrums are so silly. And so is pouting. So, of course, is whining. When we lose
our tempers, we say things that we shouldn't
say, and we do things that we shouldn't do.
Too bad!

The Bible tells us that it is foolish to
become angry and that it is wise to remain
calm. That's why we should learn to control
our tempers before our tempers control us.

Anger is the noise of the soul; the unseen irritant of the heart; the relentless invader of silence.

Max Lucado

When you lose your temper . . . you lose.

Jim Gallery

Kid-Tip

No more temper tantrums! If you think you're about to throw a tantrum, slow down, catch your breath, and walk away if you must. It's better to walk away than it is to strike out in anger.

A Prayer for Today

Lord, when I become angry, help me to remember that You offer me peace. Let me turn to You for wisdom, for patience, and for the peace that only You can give. Amen

JUST TRY YOUR BEST

Whatever you do, work at it with all your heart, as working for the Lord, not for men.

Colossians 3:23 NIV

If you're trying to be perfect, you're trying to do something that's impossible. No matter how much you try, you can't be a perfect person . . . and that's okay.

God doesn't expect you to live a mistake-free life—and neither should you. In the game of life, God expects you to try, but He doesn't always expect you to win. Sometimes, you'll make mistakes, but even then, you shouldn't give up!

So remember this: you don't have to be perfect to be a wonderful person. In fact, you don't even need to be "almost-perfect." You simply must try your best and leave the rest up to God.

94

Do we so appreciate the marvelous salvation of Jesus Christ that we are our utmost for His highest?

Oswald Chambers

Few things fire up a person's commitment like dedication to excellence.

John Maxwell

Kid-Tip

Wherever You Happen to Be, Be the Best You Can Be: Excellence is habit-forming, so give your best in everything you do.

A Prayer for Today

Dear Lord, I will strive to become a person of dedication and skill. Today, I will do my best, and I will help my friends do the same. Amen

DAY 45

THERE'S A TIME FOR EVERYTHING

There is a time for everything,
and a season for every activity under heaven.
Ecclesiastes 3:1 NIV

We human beings can be so impatient. We know what we want, and we know exactly when we want it: RIGHT NOW! But, God knows better. He has created a world that unfolds according to His own time-table, not ours.

As Christians, we must be patient as we wait for God to show us the wonderful plans that He has in store for us. And while we're waiting for God to make His plans clear, let's keep praying and keep giving thanks to the One who has given us more blessings than we can count.

The God who gives the flowers their beauty and the birds their daily food also gives His people all that they need, just when they need it.

Warren Wiersbe

Will not the Lord's time be better than your time?

C. H. Spurgeon

Kid-Tip

Big, bigger, and very big plans. God has very big plans in store for your life, so trust Him and wait patiently for those plans to unfold. And remember: God's timing is best.

A Prayer for Today

Dear Lord, sometimes I become impatient for things to happen. Help me to remember, Lord, that Your plan is best for me, not just for today, but for all eternity. Amen

DAY 46

HONESTY IS A HABIT!

We must not become tired of doing good.

Galatians 6:2 ICB

Our lives are made up of lots and lots of habits. And the habits we choose help determine the kind of people we become. If we choose habits that are good, we are happier and healthier. If we choose habits that are bad, then it's too bad for us!

Honesty, like so many other things, is a habit. And it's a habit that is right for you.

Do you want to grow up to become the kind of person that God intends for you to be? Then get into the habit of being honest with everybody. You'll be glad you did . . . and so will God!

The simple fact is that if we sow a lifestyle that is in direct disobedience to God's reveled Word, we ultimately reap disaster.

Charles Swindoll

Prayer is a habit. Worship is a habit. Kindness is a habit. And if you want to please God, you'd better make sure that these habits are your habits.

Marie T. Freeman

Kid-Tip

Choose all your habits carefully: habits are easier to make than they are to break, so be careful!

A Prayer for Today

Dear Lord, help me to be an honest person all the time, not just some of the time. And let the things that I say and do be pleasing to You this day and every day. Amen

DAY 47

SMILING IS GOOD

*Jacob said, "For what a relief it is to see
your friendly smile.
It is like seeing the smile of God!"*
Genesis 33:10 NLT

The Bible tells us that a cheerful heart is like medicine: it makes us feel better. Where does cheerfulness begin? It begins inside each of us; it begins in the heart. So let's be thankful to God for His blessings, and let's show our thanks by sharing good cheer wherever we go.

Today, make sure that you share a smile and a kind word with as many people as you can. This old world needs all the cheering up it can get . . . and so do your friends.

Life goes on. Keep on smiling and the whole world smiles with you.

Dennis Swanberg

The people whom I have seen succeed best in life have always been cheerful and hopeful people who went about their business with a smile on their faces.

Charles Kingsley

Kid-Tip

Smile as much as you can. It's good for your health, and it makes those around you feel better.

A Prayer for Today

Dear Lord, put a smile on my face, and let me share that smile with my friends and family. Amen

TOO MUCH STUFF?

Don't be obsessed with getting more material things. Be relaxed with what you have.

Hebrews 13:5 MSG

How much stuff is too much stuff? Well, if your desire for stuff is getting in the way of your desire to know God, then you've got too much stuff—it's as simple as that.

If you find yourself worrying too much about stuff, it's time to change the way you think about the things you own. Stuff isn't really very important to God, and it shouldn't be too important to you.

If you want to be truly happy, you won't find it on an endless quest for more stuff. You'll find it in receiving God's generosity and in passing that generosity along.

Bill Hybels

Kid-Tip

If you find yourself focusing too much on stuff, try spending a little less time at the mall and a little more time talking to God. Remember this fact: too much stuff doesn't ensure happiness. In fact, having too much stuff can actually prevent happiness.

A Prayer for Today

Dear God, help me remember that the stuff I own isn't very important. What's really important is the love that I feel in my heart for my family, the love that I feel for Jesus, and the love that I feel for You. Amen

WHAT JAMES SAID

This royal law is found in the Scriptures:
"Love your neighbor as yourself."
If you obey this law, then you are doing right.

James 2:8 ICB

James was the brother of Jesus and a leader of the early Christian church. In a letter that is now a part of the New Testament, James reminded his friends of a "royal law." That law is the Golden Rule.

When we treat others in the same way that we wish to be treated, we are doing the right thing. James knew it and so, of course, did his brother Jesus. Now we should learn the same lesson: it's nice to be nice; it's good to be good; and it's great to be kind.

Inasmuch as love grows in you, so beauty grows. For love is the beauty of the soul.

St. Augustine

After the forgiving comes laughter, a deeper love—and further opportunities to forgive.

Ruth Bell Graham

Kid-Tip

Kind is as kind does: In order to be a kind person, you must do kind things. Thinking about them isn't enough. So get busy! Your family and friends need all the kindness they can get!

A Prayer for Today

Dear Lord, it's easy to be kind to some people and difficult to be kind to others. Let me be kind to all people so that I might follow in the footsteps of Your Son. Amen

DAY 50

WHEN YOU'RE WORRIED

Jesus said, "Don't let your hearts be troubled.
Trust in God, and trust in me."

John 14:1 NCV

When you're worried, it helps to talk about the things that are troubling you. And who can you talk to? Well for starters, you can talk to your parents and you can talk to God.

If you're worried about something, you can pray about it any time you want. And remember that God is always listening, and He always wants to hear from you.

So when you're worried, try this plan: talk and pray. Talk to the grownups who love you, and pray to the Heavenly Father who made you. The more you talk and the more you pray, the better you'll feel.

Worry is a complete waste of energy. It solves nothing. And it won't solve that anxiety on your mind either.

Charles Swindoll

Submit each day to God, knowing that He is God over all your tomorrows.

Kay Arthur

Kid-Tip

Worried about something you said or did? If you made a mistake yesterday, the day to fix it is today. Then, you won't have to worry about it tomorrow.

A Prayer for Today

Dear Lord, when I am worried, I know where to turn for help: to those who love me, and to You. Thank You for the people who love and care for me, and thank You, Lord, for Your love. Because of that love, I have hope and assurance for this day and every day. Amen

JESUS LOVES YOU

I have loved you even as the Father has loved me. Remain in my love.
John 15:9 NLT

You've probably heard the song "Jesus Loves Me." And exactly how much does He love you? He loves you so much that He gave His life so that you might live forever with Him in heaven.

How can you repay Christ's love? By accepting Him into your heart and by obeying His rules. When you do, He will love you and bless you today, tomorrow, and forever.

Christ Jesus is the purest gold, light without darkness, bright glory unclouded. He is altogether lovely.

C. H. Spurgeon

Jesus: the proof of God's love.

Philip Yancey

Kid-Tip

Jesus loves you . . . His love is amazing, it's wonderful, and it's meant for you. His love lasts forever.

A Prayer for Today

Dear Jesus, I know that You love me today and that You will love me forever. And I thank You for Your love . . . today and forever. Amen

HONESTY AT HOME

You must choose for yourselves today whom you will serve . . . as for me and my family, we will serve the Lord.

Joshua 24:15 NCV

Should you be honest with your parents? Certainly. With your brothers and sisters? Of course. With cousins, grandparents, aunts, and uncles? Yes! In fact, you should be honest with everybody in your family because honesty starts at home.

If you can't be honest in your own house, how can you expect to be honest in other places, like at church or at school. So make sure that you're completely honest with your family. If you are, then you're much more likely to be honest with everybody else.

The single most important element in any human relationship is honesty—with oneself, with God, and with others.

Catherine Marshall

Kid-Tip

Talk about your feelings. If something is bothering you, tell your parents. Don't be afraid to talk about your feelings. Your mom and dad love you, and they can help you. So whatever "it" is, talk about it . . . with your parents!

A Prayer for Today

Heavenly Father, help me be honest with everybody, especially my family members. Make my words true and helpful, now and always. Amen

WHEN PEOPLE CAN'T HELP THEMSELVES

*I tell you the truth, whatever you did
for one of the least of these brothers of mine,
you did for me.*

Matthew 25:40 NIV

Perhaps you have lots of advantages. Some people don't. Perhaps you have the benefit of a loving family, a strong faith in God, and three good meals each day. Some people don't. Perhaps you were lucky enough to be born into a country where people are free. Some people weren't.

Jesus instructed us to care for those who can't care for themselves, wherever they may be. And, when we do something nice for someone in need, we have also done a good deed for our Savior. So today, look for someone who needs your help, and then do your best to help him or her.

People don't care how much you know until they know how much you care.

John Maxwell

We must learn to regard people less in the light of what they do or do not do, and more in the light of what they suffer.

Dietrich Bonhoeffer

Kid-Tip

When you are old enough to start giving? If you're old enough to understand these words, you're old enough to start giving to your church and to those who are less fortunate than you. If you're not sure about the best way to do it, ask your parents!

A Prayer for Today

Dear Lord, You have given me so many blessings. Make me a cheerful, generous giver, Lord, as I share the blessings that You first shared with me. Amen

GOD FIRST

Jesus answered, "'Love the Lord your God with all your heart, all your soul, and all your mind.' This is the first and most important command."

Matthew 22:37-38 NCV

Are you willing to put God first, or do you put other things ahead of your love for Him? God wants you to love Him first, and He wants you to obey Him first. When you do these things, you'll be happy you did!

When the Pharisees quizzed Jesus about God's most important commandment, Jesus answered, "Love the Lord your God with all your heart, all your soul, and all your mind. This is the first and most important command" (Matthew 22:37-38 NCV). So if you want to do the right thing, always put Him in the place He deserves: first place.

It takes all time and eternity to know God.

Oswald Chambers

God can see clearly no matter how dark or foggy the night is. Trust His Word to guide you safely home.

Lisa Whelchel

Kid-Tip

Talk to your parents about some of the ways you can put God in first place.

A Prayer for Today

Dear Lord, it's easy to talk about putting You first, but it's harder to do it in real life. Please help me put You first—really first—and not just talk about it. Amen

DAY 55

LISTENING TO GOD

The thing you should want most is
God's kingdom and doing what God wants.
Then all these other things you need
will be given to you.

Matthew 6:33 ICB

God has a perfect idea of the kind of people He wants us to become. And for starters, He wants us to be loving, kind, and patient—not rude or mean!

The Bible tells us that God is love and that if we wish to know Him, we must have love in our hearts. Sometimes, of course, when we're tired, angry, or frustrated, it is very hard for us to be loving. Thankfully, anger and frustration are feelings that come and go, but God's love lasts forever.

If you'd like to become a more patient person, talk to God in prayer, listen to what He says, and share His love with your family and friends.

In the soul-searching of our lives, we are to stay quiet so we can hear Him say all that He wants to say to us in our hearts.

Charles Swindoll

Half an hour of listening is essential except when one is very busy. Then, a full hour is needed.

St. Francis of Sales

Kid-Tip

Quiet please! This world is LOUD! To hear what God has to say, you'll need to turn down the music and turn off the television long enough for God to get His message through.

A Prayer for Today

Dear Lord, help me remember the importance of prayer. You always hear my prayers, God; let me always pray them! Amen

DAY 56

LOVE YOUR ENEMIES

I tell you, love your enemies.
Pray for those who hurt you. If you do this,
you will be true sons of your Father in heaven.
Matthew 6:44-45 ICB

It's easy to love people who have been nice to you, but it's very hard to love people who have treated you badly. Still, Jesus instructs us to treat both our friends and our enemies with kindness and respect.

Are you having problems being nice to someone? Is there someone you know whom you don't like very much? Remember that Jesus not only forgave His enemies, He also loved them . . . and so should you.

When you agree to let God love the unlovely through you, He never fails to make the unlovely lovely to you.

Beth Moore

Forgiveness is the precondition of love.

Catherine Marshall

Kid-Tip

Making up may not be as hard as you think! If there is someone who has been mean to you, perhaps it's time for the two of you to make up. If you're willing to be the first person to offer a kind word, you'll discover that making up is usually easier than you think.

A Prayer for Today

Dear Lord, give me a forgiving heart. When I have bad feelings toward another person, help me to forgive them and to love them, just as You forgive and love me. Amen

DAY 57

CHOOSE A GOOD ATTITUDE

*Your attitude should be the same that
Christ Jesus had.*
Philippians 2:5 NLT

God knows everything about you, including your attitude. And when your attitude is good, God is pleased . . . very pleased.

Are you interested in pleasing God? Are you interested in pleasing your parents? Your teachers? And your friends? If so, try to make your attitude the best it can be. When you try hard to have a good attitude, you'll make other people feel better—and you'll make yourself feel better, too.

Often, attitude is the only difference between success and failure.

John Maxwell

We must admit that we spend more of our time concentrating and fretting over the things that can't be changed than we do giving attention to the one thing we can change: our choice of attitude.

Charles Swindoll

Kid-Tip

Learn about Jesus and His attitude. Then try to do what Jesus would do.

A Prayer for Today

Dear Lord, I pray for an attitude that pleases You. Even when I'm angry, unhappy, tired, or upset, I pray that I can remember what it means to be a good person and a good Christian. Amen

PRAYING FOR PATIENCE

Do not worry about anything.
But pray and ask God for everything you need.

Philippians 4:6 ICB

Would you like to become a more patient person? Pray about it. Is there a person you don't like? Pray for a forgiving heart. Do you lose your temper more than you should? Ask God for help.

Whatever you need, ask God to help you. And, as you pray more, you'll discover that God is always near and that He's always ready to hear from you. So don't worry about things; pray about them. God is waiting . . . and listening!

God insists that we ask, not because He needs to know our situation, but because we need the spiritual discipline of asking.

Catherine Marshall

Prayer is a long rope with a strong hold.

Harriet Beecher Stowe

Kid-Tip

Pray early and often: One way to make sure that your heart is in tune with God is to pray often. The more you talk to God, the more He will talk to you.

A Prayer for Today

Dear Lord, You are always near; let me talk with You often. When I am impatient, let me turn to You. And, let me use prayer to find the peace that You desire for my life today and every day. Amen

IT'S IMPORTANT TO BE HONEST

Good people will be guided by honesty.
Proverbs 11:3 ICB

It's important to be honest. When you tell the truth, you'll feel better about yourself, and other people will feel better about you, too. But that's not all. When you tell the truth, God knows—and He will reward you for your honesty.

Telling the truth is hard sometimes. But it's better to be honest, even when it's hard. So remember this: telling the truth is always the right thing to do . . . always.

Those who are given to white lies soon become color blind.

Anonymous

We can teach our children that being honest protects from guilt and provides for a clear conscience.

Josh McDowell

Kid-Tip

If you know what's right and do what's right, you'll be a happier person. Honest and good behavior make you happier—and bad behavior doesn't. Behave accordingly.

A Prayer for Today

Dear Lord, help me be a person whose words are true and whose heart is pure. In everything that I do, let me use Jesus as my model and my guide, today and always. Amen

DOING WHAT'S RIGHT

*Doing what is right brings freedom
to honest people.*
Proverbs 11:6 ICB

Sometimes, it's so much easier to do the wrong thing than it is to do the right thing, especially when we're tired or frustrated. But, doing the wrong thing almost always leads to trouble. And sometimes, it leads to BIG trouble.

When you do the right thing, you don't have to worry about what you did or what you said. But, when you do the wrong thing, you'll be worried that someone will find out. So do the right thing, which, by the way, also happens to be the kind thing. You'll be glad you did, and so will other people!

When we do what is right, we have content-ment, peace, and happiness.

Beverly LaHaye

There may be no trumpet sound or loud applause when we make a right decision, just a calm sense of resolution and peace.

Gloria Gaither

Kid-Tip

Think ahead: Before you do something, ask yourself this question: "Will I be ashamed if my parents find out?" If the answer to that question is "Yes," don't do it!

A Prayer for Today

Dear Lord, I want to be a person who respects others, and I want to be a person who is kind. Wherever I am and whatever I do, let me be like Jesus in the way that I treat others, because with Him as my guide, I will do the right thing, today and forever. Amen

DAY 61

WHEN YOU'RE ANGRY

*A person who does not quickly get angry
shows that he has understanding.
But a person who quickly loses his temper
shows his foolishness.*

Proverbs 14:29 ICB

When you're angry, you will be tempted to say things and do things that you'll regret later. But don't do them! Instead of doing things in a hurry, slow down long enough to calm yourself down.

Jesus does not intend that you strike out against other people, and He doesn't intend that your heart be troubled by anger. Your heart should instead be filled with love, just like Jesus' heart was . . . and is!

Take no action in a furious passion. It's putting to sea in a storm.

Thomas Fuller

No one heals himself by wounding another.

St. Ambrose

Kid-Tip

Time out! If you become angry, the time to step away from the situation is before you say unkind words or do unkind things—not after. It's perfectly okay to place yourself in "time out" until you can calm down.

A Prayer for Today

Dear Lord, help me not to be an angry person, but instead, make me a forgiving person. Fill my heart not with anger, but with love for others . . . and for You. Amen

DAY 62

MAKE THE RIGHT FRIENDS

A friend loves you all the time.
Proverbs 17:17 ICB

One way that you can feel better about yourself is by staying out of trouble. And one way that you can stay out of trouble is by making friends with people who, like you, want to do what's right.

Are your friends the kind of kids who encourage you to behave yourself? If so, you've chosen your friends wisely. But if your friends try to get you in trouble, perhaps it's time to think long and hard about making some new friends.

Whether you know it or not, you're probably going to behave like your friends behave. So pick out friends who make you want to behave better, not worse. When you do, you'll feel better about yourself.

Do you want to be wise? Choose wise friends.

Charles Swindoll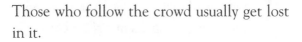

Those who follow the crowd usually get lost in it.

Rick Warren

If you try to be everything to everybody, you will end up being nothing to anybody.

Vance Havner

Kid-Tip

You simply cannot please everybody. So here's what you should do: Try pleasing God and your parents.

A Prayer for Today

Dear Lord, help me remember that I don't have to please everybody . . . but that I should always try to please You! Amen

SAY A KIND WORD

The right word spoken at the right time is as beautiful as gold apples in a silver bowl.

Proverbs 25:11 ICB

How hard is it to speak with kind words? Not very! Yet sometimes we're so busy that we forget to say the very things that might make other people feel better.

We should always try to say nice things to our families and friends. And when we feel like saying something that's not so nice, perhaps we should stop and think before we say it. Kind words help; cruel words hurt. It's as simple as that. And, when we say the right thing at the right time, we give a gift that can change someone's day or someone's life.

As you're rushing through life, take time to stop a moment, look into people's eyes, say something kind, and try to make them laugh!

Barbara Johnson

How many people stop because so few say, "Go!"

Charles Swindoll

Kid-Tip

If you don't know what to say . . . don't say anything. Sometimes, a hug works better than a whole mouthful of words.

A Prayer for Today

Dear Lord, help me to say the right thing at the right time. Let me choose my words carefully so that I can help other people and glorify You. Amen

AVOIDING QUARRELS

*Foolish people are always getting into quarrels,
but avoiding quarrels will bring you honor.*

Proverbs 20:3 ICB

In Proverbs, King Solomon gave us wonderful advice for living wisely. Solomon warned that impatience and anger lead only to trouble. And he was right!

The next time you're tempted to say an unkind word or to start an argument, remember Solomon. He was one of the wisest men who ever lived, and he knew that it's always better to be patient. So remain calm, and remember that patience is best. After all, if it's good enough for a wise man like Solomon, it should be good enough for you, too.

Argument is the worst sort of conversation.

Jonathan Swift

The Gospel has to be experienced, not argued!

Grady Nutt

You don't have to attend every argument you're invited to!

Anonymous

Kid-Tip

Tempted to fight? Walk away. The best fights are those that never happen.

A Prayer for Today

Dear Lord, when I become angry, help me to remember that You offer me peace. Let me turn to You for wisdom, for patience, and for the peace that only You can give. Amen

DAY 65

CHANGING BAD HABITS

*But wisdom will help you be good
and do what is right.*

Proverbs 2:20 NCV

Most people have a few habits they'd like to change, and maybe you do, too. If so, God can help.

If you trust God, and if you keep asking Him to help you change bad habits, He will help you make yourself into a new, smarter, more patient person. So, if at first you don't succeed, keep praying. God is listening, and He's ready to help you become a better person if you ask Him . . . so ask Him!

The simple fact is that if we sow a lifestyle that is in direct disobedience to God's Word, we ultimately reap disaster.

Charles Swindoll

You will never change your life until you change something you do daily.

John Maxwell

Kid-Tip

Choose Your Habits Carefully: Habits are easier to make than they are to break, so be careful!

A Prayer for Today

Dear Lord, help me form good habits. And let me make a habit of sharing the things that I own and the love that I feel in my heart. Amen

BEING HONEST AND KIND

Don't ever stop being kind and truthful.
Let kindness and truth show in all you do.

Proverbs 3:3 ICB

Honesty and kindness should go hand in hand. In other words, we shouldn't use honesty as an excuse to hurt other people's feelings.

It's easy to find faults in other people, and easy to tease other people about their short-comings. But it's wrong. When we needlessly hurt other people's feelings, we are disobeying God.

The Bible tells us that we should never stop being kind and truthful. And, that's very good advice for caring, thoughtful Christians . . . like you!

Be so preoccupied with good will that you haven't room for ill will.

E. Stanley Jones

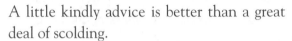

A little kindly advice is better than a great deal of scolding.

Fanny Crosby

Kid-Tip

Don't be cruel: Sometimes, you can be too honest, especially if you say unkind things that are intended to hurt other people's feelings. When you're deciding what to say, you should mix honesty and courtesy. When you do, you'll say the right thing.

A Prayer for Today

Dear Lord, help me to be a person who is both honest and kind. Let my words be truthful and encouraging. Let me always remember the Golden Rule, and let me speak accordingly. Amen

YOU'RE SPECIAL

For you made us only a little lower than God,
and you crowned us with glory and honor.
Psalm 8:5 NLT

When God made you, He made you in a very special way. In fact, you're a wonderful, one-of-a-kind creation, a special person unlike any other.

Do you realize how special you are? Do you know that God loves you because of who you are? And do you know that God has important things for you to do? Whether you realize it or not, all these things are all true.

So the next time you feel bad about something you've done, take a look in the mirror, and remember that you're looking at a wonderfully special person . . . you!

God loves you; your parents love you; your family loves you . . . and that's the way that you should feel about yourself, too.

You are valuable just because you exist. Not because of what you do or what you have done, but simply because you are.

Max Lucado

As you and I lay up for ourselves living, lasting treasures in Heaven, we come to the awesome conclusion that we ourselves are His treasure!

Anne Graham Lotz

Kid-Tip

God loves you for who you are, not because of the things you've done. So open your heart to God's love . . . when you do, you'll feel better about everything, including yourself.

A Prayer for Today

Dear Lord, You only made one me, and I know that You love me very, very much. I thank You for Your love, Lord, and I thank You for the gift of Your Son Jesus. Amen

DAY 68

WHEN THINGS GO WRONG

Be patient when trouble comes.
Pray at all times.
Romans 12:12 ICB

From time to time, all of us have to face troubles and disappointments. When we do, God is always ready to protect us. Psalm 147 promises, "He heals the brokenhearted" (v. 3 NIV), but it doesn't say that He heals them instantly. Usually, it takes time for God to heal His children.

If you find yourself in any kind of trouble, pray about it and ask God for help. And then be patient. God will work things out, just as He has promised, but He will do it in His own time and according to His own plan.

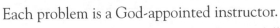
Each problem is a God-appointed instructor.

Charles Swindoll

God is bigger than your problems. Whatever worries press upon you today, put them in God's hands and leave them there.

Billy Graham

Kid-Tip

You can make it right . . . if you think you can! If you've made a mistake, apologize. If you've broken something, fix it. If you've hurt someone's feelings, apologize. If you failed at something, try again. There is always something you can do to make things better . . . so do it!

A Prayer for Today

Dear Lord, sometimes life is so hard, but with You, there is always hope. Keep me mindful that there is nothing that will happen today that You and I can't handle together. Amen

YOU DON'T HAVE TO BE PERFECT

All have sinned and are not good enough for God's glory.
Romans 3:23 NCV

If you're trying to be perfect (or if you're trying to be perfectly patient), you're trying to do something that's impossible. No matter how much you try, you can't be a perfect person . . . and that's okay.

God doesn't expect you to live a life without making any mistakes—and neither should you. In the game of life, God expects you to try, but He doesn't always expect you to win. Sometimes, you'll make mistakes, but even then, you shouldn't give up!

So remember this: you don't have to be perfect to be a wonderful person. In fact, you don't even need to be "almost-perfect." You simply must try your best and leave the rest up to God.

What makes a Christian a Christian is not perfection but forgiveness.

Max Lucado

God is so inconceivably good. He's not looking for perfection. He already saw it in Christ. He's looking for affection.

Beth Moore

Kid-Tip

If you hear a little voice inside your head telling you that you'll never be good enough . . . don't pay attention to that little voice. God loves you . . . and if you're good enough for God, you're good enough.

A Prayer for Today

Dear Lord, help me remember that I don't have to be perfect to be wonderful. Amen

THE BEST POLICY

*In every way be an example
of doing good deeds.*
Titus 2:7 NCV

Maybe you've heard this phrase: "Honesty is the best policy." And, of course, it is the best policy, but more importantly, it is also God's policy.

If we want to please God, we must honor Him by obeying His commandments. He has commanded us to be honest with everybody. Truth is God's way, and it must be our way, too.

A lie is like a snowball: the further you roll it, the bigger it becomes.

Martin Luther

The single most important element in any human relationship is honesty—with oneself, with God, and with others.

Catherine Marshall

Kid-Tip

Honesty is the best policy. Make sure that it's your policy, even when telling the truth makes you feel a little uncomfortable.

A Prayer for Today

Dear Lord, the Bible teaches me that honesty is the best policy. Help me remember that lesson today and every day of my life. Amen

DAY 71

WHEN YOU HELP OTHER PEOPLE

So let us try to do what makes peace and helps one another.
Romans 14:19 NCV

Sometimes we would like to help make the world a better place, but we're not sure how to do it. Jesus told the story of the "Good Samaritan," a man who helped a fellow traveler when no one else would. We, too, should be good Samaritans when we find people who need our help. A good place to start helping other people is at home. You can also help at school and at church.

Another way that we can help other people is to pray for them. God always hears our prayers, so we should talk with Him as often as we can. When we do, we're not only doing a wonderful thing for the people we pray for, we're also doing a wonderful thing for ourselves, too.

Make it a rule, and pray to God to help you to keep it, never, if possible, to lie down at night without being able to say: "I have made one human being at least a little wiser, or a little happier, or at least a little better this day."

Charles Kingsley

Kid-Tip

Someone very near you may need a helping hand or a kind word, so keep your eyes open, and look for people who need your help, whether at home, at church, or at school.

A Prayer for Today

Dear Lord, let me help others in every way that I can. Jesus served others; I can too. I will serve other people with my good deeds and with my prayers, and I will give thanks for all those who serve and protect our nation and our world. Amen

ALWAYS GROWING UP

*But grow in the special favor and knowledge of
our Lord and Savior Jesus Christ.
To him be all glory and honor,
both now and forevermore. Amen.*

2 Peter 3:18 NLT

When do we stop growing up? Hopefully never! If we keep studying God's Word, and if we obey His commandments, we will never be "fully grown" Christians. We will always be growing.

God intends that we continue growing in the love and knowledge of Christ. And when we do so, we become more patient, more loving, more understanding, and more Christlike. And we keep growing and growing . . . and growing!

Trying to grow up hurts. You make mistakes. You try to learn from them, and when you don't, it hurts even more.

Aretha Franklin

Don't go through life, grow through life.

Eric Butterworth

Kid-Tip

Read the Bible? Yes! Try to read the Bible with your parents every day. If they forget, remind them!

A Prayer for Today

Dear Lord, let me keep learning about Your love and Your Son as long as I live. Make me a better person today than I was yesterday, but not as good a person as I can become tomorrow if I continue to trust in You. Amen

KNOW JESUS, KNOW PEACE

Let the peace of Christ rule in your hearts,
since as members of one body
you were called to peace.
Colossians 3:15 NIV

Jesus offers us peace . . . peace in our hearts and peace in our homes. But He doesn't force us to enjoy His peace—we can either accept His peace or not.

When we accept the peace of Jesus Christ by opening up our hearts to Him, we feel much better about ourselves, our families, and our lives.

Would you like to feel a little better about yourself and a little better about your corner of the world? Then open up your heart to Jesus, because that's where real peace—and real truth—begins.

In the center of a hurricane there is absolute quiet and peace. There is no safer place than in the center of the will of God.

Corrie ten Boom

The secret of the Christian is that he knows the absolute deity of the Lord Jesus Christ.

Oswald Chambers

Kid-Tip

God's peace can be yours right now. . . if you open up your heart and invite Him in.

A Prayer for Today

Dear Lord, I will open my heart to You. And I thank You, God, for Your love, for Your peace, and for Your Son. Amen

LAUGHTER IS A GOOD THING

There is a time for everything,
and everything on earth has its special season.
There is a time to cry and a time to laugh.
There is a time to be sad and a time to dance.

Ecclesiastes 3:1, 4 NCV

Do you like to laugh? Of course you do! Laughter is a gift from God that He hopes you'll use in the right way. So here are a few things to remember:

1. God wants you to be happy. 2. Laughter is a good thing when you're laughing at the right things. 3. You should laugh with people, but you should never laugh at them.

God created laughter for a reason . . . and God knows best. So do yourself a favor: laugh at the right things . . . and laugh a lot!

Laughter is the language of the young at heart and the antidote to what ails us.

Barbara Johnson

If you can laugh at yourself loudly and often, you will find it liberating. There's no better way to prevent stress from becoming distress.

John Maxwell

Kid-Tip

Laughter is good medicine. So here's your prescription: Laugh lots!

A Prayer for Today

Dear Lord, laughter is Your gift. Today and every day, put a smile on my face, and let me share that smile with all who cross my path . . . and let me laugh. Amen

BEING KIND TO PARENTS

Honor your father and your mother.
Exodus 20:12 ICB

We love our parents so very much, but sometimes, we may take them for granted. When we take them "for granted," that means that we don't give them the honor and respect they deserve.

The Bible tells us to honor our parents. That's God's rule, and it's also the best way to live. When we treat our parents with the respect they deserve, we show them that we appreciate all they have done for us. And that's so much better than taking our parents for granted. If you don't believe it, just ask them!

What lessons about honor did you learn from your childhood? Are you living what you learned today?

Dennis Swanberg

Parents can tell but never teach until they practice what they preach.

Anonymous

Kid-Tip

Two magic words: Thank you! Your parents will never become tired of hearing those two little words. And while you're at it, try three more: "I love you!"

A Prayer for Today

Dear Lord, make me respectful and thankful. Let me give honor and love to my parents, and let my behavior be pleasing to them . . . and to You. Amen

THE TRUTH ACCORDING TO JESUS

So Jesus said to the Jews who believed in him, "If you continue to obey my teaching, you are truly my followers. Then you will know the truth. And the truth will make you free.

John 8:31-32 ICB

Jesus had a message for all of His followers. He said, "The truth will set you free." When we do the right thing and tell the truth, we don't need to worry about our lies catching up with us. When we behave honestly, we don't have to worry about feeling guilty or ashamed. But, if we fail to do what we know is right, bad things start to happen, and we feel guilty.

Jesus understood that the truth is a very good thing indeed. We should understand it, too. And, we should keep telling it as long as we live.

Freedom is not the right to do what we want but the power to do what we ought.

Corrie ten Boom

The only source of Life is the Lord Jesus Christ.

Oswald Chambers

Kid-Tip

The Truth with a capital "T": Jesus is the Truth with a capital "T" . . . and that's the truth!

A Prayer for Today

Dear Lord, thank You for Your Son Jesus. Let Him be the light of my life, the Savior of my soul, and the model for my behavior. Amen

BLESS OTHERS

If you have two shirts,
share with the person who does not have one.
If you have food, share that too.

Luke 3:11 ICB

Lots of people in the world aren't as fortunate as you are. Some of these folks live in far-away places, and that makes it harder to help them. But other people who need your help are living very near you.

Ask your parents to help you find ways to do something nice for folks who need it. And don't forget that everybody needs love, kindness, and respect, so you should always be ready to share those things, too.

It doesn't take monumental feats to make the world a better place. It can be as simple as letting someone go ahead of you in a grocery line.

Barbara Johnson

Kid-Tip

Too many toys? Give them away! Are you one of those lucky kids who has more toys than you can play with? If so, remember that not everyone is so lucky. Ask your parents to help you give some of your toys to children who need them more than you do.

A Prayer for Today

Dear Lord, I know there is no happiness in keeping Your blessings for myself. Today, I will share my blessings with my family, with my friends, and with people who need my help. Amen

HOW TO BE HAPPY

*Those who want to do right more than
anything else are happy.*
Matthew 5:6 ICB

Do you want to be happy? Here are some things you should do: Love God and His Son, Jesus; obey the Golden Rule; and always try to do the right thing. When you do these things, you'll discover that happiness goes hand-in-hand with good behavior.

The happiest people do not misbehave; the happiest people are not cruel or greedy. The happiest people don't say unkind things. The happiest people are those who love God and follow His rules—starting, of course, with the Golden one.

Learning how to forgive and forget is one of the secrets of a happy Christian life.

Warren Wiersbe

Kid-Tip

Sometimes Happy, Sometimes Not: Even if you're a very good person, you shouldn't expect to be happy all the time. Sometimes, things will happen to make you sad, and it's okay to be sad when bad things happen to you or to your friends and family. But remember: through good times and bad, you'll always be happier if you obey the rules of your Father in heaven. So obey them!

A Prayer for Today

Dear Lord, make me the kind of Christian who earns happiness by doing the right thing. When I obey Your rules, Father, I will find the joy that You have in store for me. Let me find Your joy, Lord, today and always. Amen

DAY 79

PAUL AND HIS FRIENDS

I thank my God every time I remember you.
Philippians 1:3 NIV

In his letter to the Philippians, Paul wrote to his distant friends saying that he thanked God every time he remembered them. We, too, should thank God for the family and friends He has brought into our lives.

Today, let's give thanks to God for all the people who love us, for brothers and sisters, parents and grandparents, aunts and uncles, cousins, and friends. And then, as a way of thanking God, let's obey Him by being especially kind to our loved ones. They deserve it, and so does He.

God often keeps us on the path by guiding us through the counsel of friends and trusted spiritual advisors.

Bill Hybels

Kid-Tip

The mailman can help: If you have friends or relatives who are far away, send them letters or drawings (your mom or dad will be happy to mail them for you). Everybody loves to receive mail, and so will your family members and friends.

A Prayer for Today

Dear Lord, thank You for my family and my friends. Let me show kindness to all of them: those who are here at home and those who are far away. Then my family and friends will know that I remember them and love them, today and every day. Amen

THE THINGS WE SAY

A good person's words will help many others.
Proverbs 10:21 ICB

The words that we speak are very important because of how they effect other people. The things that we say can either help people or hurt them. We can either make people feel better, or we can hurt their feelings.

The Bible reminds us that words are powerful things; we must use them carefully. Let's use our words to help our families and friends. When we do, we make their lives better as well as our own.

A little kindly advice is better than a great deal of scolding.

Fanny Crosby

Like dynamite, God's power is only latent power until it is released. You can release God's dynamite power into people's lives and the world through faith, your words, and prayer.

Bill Bright

Kid-Tip

Think first, speak second: If you want to keep from hurting other people's feelings, don't open your mouth until you've turned on your brain.

A Prayer for Today

Dear Lord, make my words pleasing to You. Let the words that I say and the things that I do help others feel better about themselves and to know more about You. Amen

SLOW DOWN

*Careful planning puts you ahead
in the long run; hurry and scurry
puts you further behind.*
Proverbs 21:5 MSG

Are you sometimes just a little bit impulsive? Do you sometimes fail to look before you leap? If so, God wants you to be a little bit more careful—or maybe a lot more careful!

The Bible makes it clear: we're supposed to behave wisely, not carelessly. But sometimes we're tempted to rush ahead and do things before we think about them.

So do yourself a big favor—slow down, think things through, and look carefully before you leap.

Some of us would do more for the Lord if we did less.

Vance Havner

To be successful, you can't just run on the fast track: run on your track.

John Maxwell

Kid-Tip

Keep your eyes and mind focused on the important things. And remember this: the most important thing is your relationship with God and His Son.

A Prayer for Today

Dear Lord, sometimes, I am distracted by the busyness of the day. When I am worried or anxious, Father, turn my thoughts back to You. Help me to trust Your will, to follow Your commands, and to accept Your peace, today and forever. Amen

THE PERSON IN THE MIRROR

*Unfailing love surrounds those
who trust the LORD.*
Psalm 32:10 NLT

Do you really like the person you see when you look into the mirror? You should! After all, the person in the mirror is a very special person who is made—and loved—by God.

In fact, you are loved in many, many ways: God loves you, your parents love you, and your family loves you, for starters. So you should love yourself, too.

So here's something to think about: since God thinks you're special, and since so many people think you're special, isn't it about time for you to agree with them? Of course it is! It's time to say, "You're very wonderful and very special," to the person you see in the mirror.

Give yourself a gift today: be present with yourself. God is. Enjoy your own personality. God does.

Barbara Johnson

Being loved by Him whose opinion matters most gives us the security to risk loving, too—even loving ourselves.

Gloria Gaither

Kid-Tip

Remember: God loves you, and lots of people love you, too . . . so it's only proper that you should admit that you're a very special person.

A Prayer for Today

Dear Lord, today and every day, I will do my best to love everybody . . . including myself. Amen

WHEN PEOPLE ARE NOT NICE

*If someone does wrong to you,
do not pay him back by doing wrong to him.*

Romans 12:17 ICB

Sometimes people aren't nice, and that's when we feel like striking back in anger. But the Bible tells us not to do it. As Christians, we should not repay one bad deed with another bad deed. Instead, we should forgive the other person as quickly as we can.

Are you angry at someone? If so, then it's time to forgive him or her. Jesus does not intend for your heart to be troubled by anger. Your heart should instead be filled with love, just as Jesus' heart was . . . and is!

We are all fallen creatures and all very hard to live with.

C. S. Lewis

You can be sure you are abiding in Christ if you are able to have a Christlike love toward the people that irritate you the most.

Vonette Bright

Kid-Tip

Forgive . . . and keep forgiving! Sometimes you may forgive someone once and then, at a later time, become angry at the very same person again. If so, you must forgive that person again and again . . . until it sticks!

A Prayer for Today

Dear Lord, whenever I am angry, give me a forgiving heart. And help me remember that the best day to forgive somebody is this one. Amen

HONESTY STARTS WITH YOU!

These are the things you must do:
Speak truth to one another; render honest
and peaceful judgments in your gates.
Zechariah 8:16 HCSB

Where does honesty begin? In your own heart and your own head. If you sincerely want to be an honest person, then you must ask God to help you find the courage and the determination to be honest all of the time.

Honesty is not a "sometimes" thing. If you intend to be a truthful person, you must make truthfulness a habit that becomes so much a part of you that you don't have to decide whether or not you're going to tell the truth. Instead, you will simply tell the truth because it's the kind of person you are.

The God who dwells in heaven is willing to dwell also in the heart of the humble believer.

Warren Wiersbe

Our actions are seen by people, but our motives are monitored by God.

Franklin Graham

Kid-Tip

How can you please your Heavenly Father? By telling the truth, by obeying your parents, and by obeying God.

A Prayer for Today

Dear Lord, You know my heart. Help me to say things, to do things, and to think things that are pleasing to You. Amen

NEED HELP? ASK GOD!

Continue to ask, and God will give to you.
Continue to search and you will find.
Continue to knock, and the door
will open for you.
Matthew 7:7 ICB

Perhaps you've tried to be more honest with other people, but you're still falling back into your old habits. If so, don't get discouraged. Instead, become even more determined to become the person God wants you to be.

If you trust God, and if you keep asking Him to help you become a more truthful person, He will help you make yourself into that person. So, if at first you don't succeed, keep praying. God is listening, and He's ready to help you change if you ask Him . . . so ask Him!

When will we realize that we're not troubling God with our questions and concerns? Our very personal God wants to hear from us personally.

Gigi Graham Tchividjian

Kid-Tip

Got Questions? Ask God! If you have a question, pray about it. Whatever your question, God has the answer, but it's up to you to ask.

A Prayer for Today

Lord, today I will ask You for the things I need. In every situation, I will come to You in prayer. You know what I want, Lord, and more importantly, You know what I need. Yet even though I know that You know, I still won't be too timid—or too busy—to ask. Amen

OBEY AND BE HAPPY

But the truly happy person is the one who carefully studies God's perfect law that makes people free. He continues to study it. He listens to God's teaching and does not forget what he heard. Then he obeys what God's teaching says. When he does this, it makes him happy.

James 1:25 ICB

Do you want to be happy? Then you should learn to obey your parents and your teachers. And, of course, you should also learn to obey God. When you do, you'll discover that happiness goes hand-in-hand with good behavior.

The happiest people do not misbehave; the happiest people are not cruel or greedy. The happiest people don't disobey their parents, their teachers, or their Father in heaven. The happiest people are those who obey the rules . . .

Happiness is obedience, and obedience is happiness.

C. H. Spurgeon

Perfect obedience would be perfect happiness, if only we had perfect confidence in the power we were obeying.

Corrie ten Boom

Kid-Tip

Good behavior leads to a happy life. And bad behavior doesn't.

A Prayer for Today

Dear Heavenly Father, when I obey, I'm a much happier person. Help me learn the importance of obeying my parents and the importance of obeying You. Amen

DAY 87

WHAT THE BIBLE SAYS ABOUT HONESTY

Your word is like a lamp for my feet
and a light for my way.
Psalm 119:105 ICB

What book contains everything that God has to say about honesty? The Bible, of course. If you read the Bible every day, you'll soon be convinced that honesty is very important to God. And, since honesty is important to God, it should be important to you, too.

The Bible is the most important book you'll ever own. It's God's Holy Word. Read it every day and follow its instructions. If you do, you'll be safe now and forever.

The Bible is God's Word to man.

Kay Arthur

If at first you don't succeed, read the Instruction Manual—God's.

Anonymous

Kid-Tip

Who's in charge of your Bible? If you're the person who's supposed to be taking care of your Bible, then take that responsibility seriously. Your Bible is by far the most important book you own!

A Prayer for Today

Dear Lord, You have given me a wonderful gift: the Holy Bible. Let me read it and understand it and follow the commandments that I find there. Amen

WHEN FRIENDS MISBEHAVE

Hate what is evil. Hold on to what is good.
Romans 12:9 ICB

When your friends misbehave or say things that aren't true, do you tell them to stop, or do you go along with the crowd? Usually, it's much easier to go along with the crowd—or to say nothing at all—but that's the wrong thing to do. It's better to stand up for what you know is right.

Sometimes, grown ups must stand up for the things they believe in. When they do, it can be hard for them, too. But the Bible tells us over and over again that we should do the right thing, not the easy thing.

God's world is a wonderful place, but people who misbehave can spoil things in a hurry. So if your friends behave poorly, don't copy them! Instead, do the right thing.

Friends are like a quilt with lots of different shapes, sizes, colors, and patterns of fabric. But the end result brings you warmth and comfort in a support system that makes your life richer and fuller.

Suzanne Dale Ezell

A true friend is the gift of God.

Robert South

Kid-Tip

If you're not sure that it's the right thing to do, don't do it! And if you're not sure that it's the truth, don't tell it.

A Prayer for Today

Dear Lord, today I will worry less about pleasing other people and more about pleasing You. Amen

IN CONTROL

*A person without self-control is as defenseless as
a city with broken-down walls.*

Proverbs 25:28 NLT

When we learn how to control ourselves,
we can be more considerate of other people.
Would you like to make the world a better
place? If so, you can start by practicing the
Golden Rule.

Jesus said, "Do to others what you want
them to do to you" (Matthew 7:12 NCV).
That means that you should treat other people in the very same way that you want to be
treated. That's the Golden Rule.

Jesus wants us to treat other people with
respect, kindness, courtesy, and love. When
we do, we make our families and our friends
happy . . . and we make our Father in heaven
very proud.

Your thoughts are the determining factor as to whose mold you are conformed to. Control your thoughts and you control the direction of your life.

Charles Stanley

If one examines the secret behind a championship football team, a magnificent orchestra, or a successful business, the principal ingredient is invariably discipline.

James Dobson

Kid-Tip

When you learn how to control yourself, you'll be happier . . . and your parents will be happier, too.

A Prayer for Today

Dear Lord, I want to be able to control myself better and better each day. Help me find better ways to behave myself that are pleasing to You. Amen

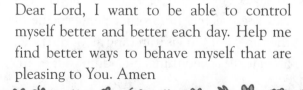

LISTENING TO YOUR CONSCIENCE

*Believe me, I do my level best to keep
a clear conscience before God and
my neighbors in everything I do.*
Acts 24:16 MSG

Sometimes, you know that something isn't the right thing to do, but you do it anyway. Even if no one else knows, you know . . . and so does God! You can keep secrets from other people, but you can't keep secrets from Him. God knows what you think and what you do.

If your heart tells you not to do something, don't do it! If your conscience tells you that something is wrong, stop! If you're tempted to say something that isn't true, don't! You can keep secrets from other people some of the time, but God is watching all of the time, and He sees everything, including your heart.

God desires that we become spiritually healthy enough through faith to have a conscience that rightly interprets the work of the Holy Spirit.

Beth Moore

Your conscience is your alarm system. It's your protection.

Charles Stanley

Kid-Tip

That little voice inside your head . . . is called your conscience. Listen to it; it's usually right!

A Prayer for Today

Dear Lord, other people see me only from the outside, but You know my heart. Let my heart be pure, and let me listen to the voice that You have placed there, today and every day that I live. Amen

WHEN MISTAKES HAPPEN

*But if we confess our sins, he will forgive
our sins. We can trust God. He does what
is right. He will make us clean from
all the wrongs that we have done.*

1 John 1:9 ICB

Do you make mistakes? We all do. Nobody is perfect, and you should not expect to be perfect, either.

When you make a mistake, the best thing to do is to admit it, to correct it, and to try very hard not to make it again. Then, your mistakes can become opportunities to learn.

Sometimes, mistakes can be the very best way to learn, so learn from them. But don't keep making the same mistake over and over again. That's not learning; that's silly!

Father, take our mistakes and turn them into opportunities.

Max Lucado

Lord, when we are wrong, make us willing to change; and when we are right, make us easy to live with.

Peter Marshall

Kid-Tip

Fix it sooner rather than later: If you make a mistake or say something that isn't true, the time to make things better is now, not later! The sooner you admit your mistake, the better.

A Prayer for Today

Dear Lord, when I make mistakes, let me admit them and correct them. When I am wrong, let me be quick to change and quick to ask forgiveness from others and from You. Amen

GOD CAN HANDLE IT

Live full lives, full in the fullness of God.
God can do anything, you know—far more
than you could ever imagine or guess or request
in your wildest dreams! He does it not by
pushing us around but by working within us,
his Spirit deeply and gently within us.

Ephesians 3:19-20 MSG

It's a promise that is made over and over again in the Bible: Whatever "it" is, God can handle it.

Life isn't always easy. Far from it! Sometimes, life can be hard, but even then, we're protected by a loving Heavenly Father. When we're worried, God can help us; when we're sad, God can comfort us. God is not just near; He is here. So we should always lift our thoughts and prayers to Him. When we do, He will answer our prayers. Why? Because He is our shepherd, and He has promised to protect us now and forever.

God's sovereignty is the attribute by which He rules His entire creation, and to be sovereign, God must be all-knowing, all-powerful, and absolutely free.

A. W. Tozer

God is in control, and therefore in everything I can give thanks, not because of the situation, but because of the One who directs and rules over it.

Kay Arthur

Kid-Tip

God's love can make everything right, including you!

A Prayer for Today

Dear Lord, You rule over our world, and I will allow You to rule over my heart. I will obey Your commandments, I will study Your Word, and I will seek Your will for my life, today and every day of my life. Amen

KIND WORDS

When you talk, do not say harmful things. But say what people need—words that will help them become stronger. Then what you say will help those who listen to you.

Ephesians 4:29 ICB

Do you like for people to say kind words to you? Of course you do! And that's exactly how other people feel, too. That's why it's so important to say things that make people feel better, not worse.

Your words can help people . . . or not. Make certain that you're the kind of person who says helpful things, not hurtful things. And, make sure that you're the kind of person who helps other people feel better about themselves, not worse.

Everybody needs to hear kind words, and that's exactly the kind of words they should hear from you!

Fill the heart with the love of Christ so that only truth and purity can come out of the mouth.

Warren Wiersbe

We will always experience regret when we live for the moment and do not weigh our words and deeds before we give them life.

Lisa Bevere

Kid-Tip

If you can't think of something nice to say . . . don't say anything. It's better to say nothing than to hurt someone's feelings.

A Prayer for Today

Dear Lord, You hear every word that I say. Help me remember to me speak words that are honest, kind, and helpful. Amen

FINISH IT

Patient endurance is what you need now, so you will continue to do God's will. Then you will receive all that he has promised.

Hebrews 10:36 NLT

If you think you can do something, then you can probably do it. If you think you can't do something, then you probably won't do it.

So remember this: if you're having a little trouble getting something done, don't get mad, don't get frustrated, don't get discouraged, and don't give up. Just keep trying . . . and believe in yourself.

When you try hard—and keep trying hard—you can really do amazing things . . . but if you quit at the first sign of trouble, you'll miss out. So here's a good rule to follow: when you have something that you want to finish, finish it . . . and finish it sooner rather than later.

Keep adding, keep walking, keep advancing; do not stop, do not turn back, do not turn from the straight road.

St. Augustine

By perseverance the snail reached the ark.

C. H. Spurgeon

Kid-Tip

If things don't work out at first, don't quit. If you don't keep trying, you'll never know how good you can be.

A Prayer for Today

Dear Lord, sometimes I feel like giving up. When I feel that way, help me do the right thing . . . and help me finish the work You want me to do. Amen

GROWING UP WITH GOD

He will teach us of his ways,
and we will walk in his paths.

Isaiah 2:3 KJV

When will you stop growing up? Hopefully never! If you keep studying God's Word and obeying His commandments, you will never be a "fully grown" Christian. You will always be a "growing" Christian.

An important part of growing up is learning that honesty is better than dishonesty and that true words are better than lies. You have already learned that lesson; now, it's time to put your knowledge to good use by doing the things that you know are right.

God knows you can't be perfect, but He doesn't want you to keep doing bad things, either! Instead, God wants you to keep growing in the love and knowledge of His Son.

God loves us the way we are, but He loves us too much to leave us that way.

Leighton Ford

As I have continued to grow in my Christian maturity, I have discovered that the Holy Spirit does not let me get by with anything.

Anne Graham Lotz

Kid-Tip

Daily devotionals? Yes! Try your best to read the Bible with your parents every day. If they forget, remind them!

A Prayer for Today

Dear Lord, let me always keep learning about Your love and about Your Son, Jesus. Make me a better person today than I was yesterday, and let me continue to grow as a Christian every day that I live. Amen

DON'T BE TOO HARD ON YOURSELF

You know the Lord is full of mercy and is kind.
James 5:11 NCV

Face facts: nobody's perfect . . . not even you! And remember this: it's perfectly okay not to be perfect. In fact, God doesn't expect you to be perfect, and you shouldn't expect yourself to be perfect, either.

Are you one of those people who can't stand to make a mistake? Do you think that you must please everybody all the time? When you make a mess of things, do you become terribly upset? Mistakes happen . . . it's simply a fact of life, and it's simply a part of growing up. So don't be too hard on yourself, especially if you've learned something along the way.

The happiest people in the world are not those who have no problems, but the people who have learned to live with those things that are less than perfect.

James Dobson

If you can forgive the person you were, accept the person you are, and believe in the person you will become, you are headed for joy. So celebrate your life.

Barbara Johnson

Kid-Tip

It's okay to be less than perfect: you don't have to be perfect to be wonderful.

A Prayer for Today

Dear Lord, help me be kind to everybody, including myself. And when I make a mistake, help me to forgive myself, just like I forgive other people when they make mistakes. Amen

GOD KNOWS

*I am the Lord, and I can look
into a person's heart.*
Jeremiah 17:10 ICB

Even when you think nobody is watching, God is. Nothing that we say or do escapes the watchful eye of our Lord. God understands that we are not perfect, but He also wants us to live according to His rules, not our own.

The next time that you're tempted to say something that you shouldn't say or to do something that you shouldn't do, remember that you can't keep secrets from God. So don't even try!

Bible history is filled with people who began the race with great success but failed at the end because they disregarded God's rules.

Warren Wiersbe

If you lack knowledge, go to school. If you lack wisdom, get on your knees.

Vance Havner

Kid-Tip

Made a mistake? Ask for forgiveness? If you've broken one of God's rules, you can always ask Him for His forgiveness. And He will always give it!

A Prayer for Today

Dear Lord, thank You for watching over me. Let the things that I say and do be pleasing to You. And Lord, thank You for Your love; let me share it with others today and every day. Amen

PEACE IS WONDERFUL

I leave you peace. My peace I give you.
I do not give it to you as the world does.
So don't let your hearts be troubled.

John 14:27 ICB

The beautiful words from John 14:27 remind us that Jesus offers us peace, not as the world gives, but as He alone gives. We, as believers, can accept His peace or ignore it. When we accept the peace of Jesus Christ into our hearts, our lives are changed forever, and we become more loving, patient Christians.

Christ's peace is offered freely; it has already been paid for; it is ours for the asking. So let us ask . . . and then share.

Peace does not mean to be in a place where there is no noise, trouble, or hard work. Peace means to be in the midst of all those things and still be calm in your heart.

Catherine Marshall

Kid-Tip

Count to ten . . . but don't stop there! If you're angry with someone, don't say the first thing that comes to your mind. Instead, catch your breath and start counting until you are once again in control of your temper. If you count to a million and you're still counting, go to bed! You'll feel better in the morning.

A Prayer for Today

Dear Lord, help me to accept Your peace and then share it with others, today and forever. Amen

PRAISE GOD

Let the godly sing with joy to the Lord,
for it is fitting to praise him.
Psalm 33:1 NLT

The Bible makes it clear: it pays to say "thank You" to God. But sometimes, we may not feel like thanking anybody, not even our Father in heaven.

If we ever stop praising God, it's a big mistake . . . a VERY BIG mistake.

When you stop to think about it, God has been very generous with you . . . and He deserves a great big "thanks" for all those amazing gifts.

Do you want an attitude that pleases God? Then make sure that your attitude praises God. And don't just praise Him on Sunday morning. Praise Him every day, starting with this one.

Our God is the sovereign Creator of the universe! He loves us as His own children and has provided every good thing we have; He is worthy of our praise every moment.

Shirley Dobson

Kid-Tip

Praise Him! One of the main reasons you go to church is to praise God. But, you don't need to wait until Sunday rolls around to thank your Heavenly Father. Instead, you  can praise Him many times each day by saying silent prayers that only He can hear.

A Prayer for Today

Heavenly Father, today and every day I will praise You. I will praise You with my thoughts, my prayers, my words, and my deeds . . . now and forever. Amen

HEAVEN

Be glad and rejoice,
because your reward is great in heaven.
Matthew 5:12 HCSB

It's time to remind yourself of a promise that God made a long time ago—the promise that God sent His Son Jesus to save the world and to save you! And when you stop to think about it, there can be no greater promise than that.

No matter where you are, God is with you. God loves you, and He sent His Son so that you can live forever in heaven with your loved ones. WOW! That's the greatest promise in the history of the universe. The end.

You can look forward with hope, because one day there will be no more separation, no more scars, and no more suffering in My Father's House. It's the home of your dreams!

Anne Graham Lotz

God's people have always tied their lives to a single hope, the assurance of one day seeing God in heaven.

Warren Wiersbe

Kid-Tip

Heaven is all those wonderful things you wish you had on earth . . . and so very much more.

A Prayer for Today

Dear Lord, I thank You for the gift of eternal life that is mine through Your Son Jesus. I will keep the promise of heaven in my heart today and every day. Amen

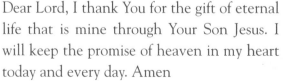